Personal Style

Original Story:
Jennifer Degenhardt

Translator:
Matías Salazar

Editor:
Lucas González

Illustrator:
A.P.

Copyright © 2025 Jennifer Degenhardt (Puentes)
All rights reserved.
ISBN: 978-1-956594-65-2

❝ Style is not about the clothes; it's about the individual. **❞**

-Alexander McQueen

TABLE OF CONTENTS

ACKNOWLEDGMENTS

In keeping with my plan, there are three students whom I would like to thank for their help in getting this story to you:

Matías Salazar, a then-seventh grader, powered through the translation of this story, getting the words down in English. Taking the reins from there was Lucas González, a high schooler, who edited the text to make it more teenager-y in English.

Finally, a shout-out to A.P., a then-eighth grader (and fashion connoisseur), who brought the story to life in images.

None of us is perfect, but each of us is perfect in our intentions. Hope you enjoy the story.

AUTHOR'S NOTE:

A reminder that this story was originally written in Spanish for language learners, and this version is a translation of the original. I hope that this story, with its simpler and more accessible vocabulary, will be a useful, fun read for English language learners.

Chapter 1
A Bad Day

It's May.

I'm at a new school.

It's my first day.

It's not the ideal time of year to be a new student at any school.

My old school had a uniform. This school doesn't have one.

But all the students sort of have a dress code: the same shirts, the same pants, and of course, the same shoes. And all the students have clothes from Under Armour and Nike.

The school does not have an official dress code, but there is an unofficial uniform.

I don't have the unofficial uniform. I don't have a shirt from Hollister, I don't have pants from Aeropostale, and I don't have shoes from Nike.

I'm different. I don't like to be different, but I am different.

I'm in class, and I hear the students talking about me.

"Look at those pants. They aren't pants from Aeropostale."

"Look at those shoes. They aren't shoes from Nike."

I don't want to be in Newport. I don't want to be at a new school. I don't want to be here. I want to be invisible.

*****

After School

I'm at the entrance of the house. I'm sad because I don't like my new school, I don't like the students, and I don't like the unofficial uniform.

I'm outside my grandma's house, but I don't have my key. I can't get inside. I'm not happy. I'm upset.

I'm very upset. I don't want to be seen by anyone, but I can't get inside the house. What a horrible day.

I write a text message to my grandma:

> *My sweet grandma, I don't have my key. I can't get inside the house.*

I start to cry a little.

At that moment, I see two people. They are walking in front of the house. One of them says to me:

"Hi! I'm Sydney. I use the pronouns she/her. You're Jayde, right?" she asks me

I'm nervous. This person knows me, but I don't know who she is.

She starts talking again.

"My name is Sydney. I'm a friend of your grandmother. This is my friend, Marley," she says.

"Hi, I'm Marley," the guy says. "I use the pronouns (he/him)."

This guy is tall, young, and has long, brown hair. He has brown eyes and a tattoo of a peace symbol on his foot. ☮

Sydney is not tall, and she is young. She has blonde hair and blue eyes. I don't see any tattoos on her.

"Hi, I'm Jayde. I use the pronouns they/them," I say with a smile.

"Nice to meet you, Jayde!"

"How do you know me?" I ask Sydney.

"Your grandmother is my friend. She talks a lot about you."

"My grandmother is your friend? My grandma is old," I tell her.

"Ha! Your grandmother is NOT old. She's young. She's friends with everyone here in the neighborhood. She's very popular."

I think about what she just said. *My grandmother? Everyone's friend? Popular? Is it possible? She is the best but... she's old!*

"Jayde, why aren't you inside the house?" asks Sydney.

"I can't get inside. I don't have my key."

"Do you want to go to the store with us? I can call your grandmother..."

Sydney calls my grandmother.

"Good idea, Sydney. Jayde, do you like clothes?" Marley asks.

"Yes, I like them. But I don't like MY clothes," says Jayde.

Sydney talks to both of us. "OK. Your grandmother says that you can come to the store with us."

"Store?" I ask them. "What store?"

"To our store, Folk Vintage. It's a vintage clothing store."

"Vintage clothes?" I ask them.

"Yes. Great clothes. Let's go" says Marley.

Chapter 2
The Jacket

We walk to the Folk Vintage store. It's a vintage clothing store on Thames Street in Newport.

Vintage clothing is clothing that is more than twenty years old. It's clothing from different time periods, like the 1970s and 1980s.

"Here we are," Sydney says. "This is our store."

Jayde enters the store. It's not a big store like DICK'S SPORTING GOODS, but it has a lot of clothes:

- shirts
- sweaters
- pants
- dresses
- skirts
- vests
- jackets
- shoes
- boots
- hats
- scarves
- hats
- T-shirts

They are not regular clothes. clothes are original. They are spectacular. They are fabulous. They are dramatic. They are magnificent and stylish. They're wonderful.

"Wow, Sydney! I really like the store, and I really like all the clothes," I say.

"Thank you, Jayde. Do you like vintage clothing?" Sydney asks.

"Yeah. The clothes are dramatic... and magnificent. They are interesting and fabulous. The clothes are original and wonderful."

Marley goes to the back room and takes out a box.

"Here are the new clothes, Syd," Marley says.

"Thank you, Marley. Let's separate the clothes now. Do you want to help, Jayde?" Sydney asks.

I don't answer. I'm so impressed by the clothes. I look everywhere in the store. I see a jacket that catches my eye. It's a white jacket with big black buttons. It's a magnificent jacket. It's unique.

At that moment, I don't think about the problems I have at school. I think about the jacket. I love it.

"Do you like that jacket, Jayde?" asks Sydney.

Sydney takes out the white jacket with black buttons and shows it to me.

I take the jacket and put it on. It's spectacular.

"Wow! I love this jacket," I tell her. "I feel very stylish in this jacket."

With the jacket on, I feel happy. I don't feel unhappy. I feel different.

I look at the price tag. The price is… oh! It's expensive. I don't have any money. I can't buy it.

"That jacket is very stylish. One day, I will buy it," I tell Sydney

Marley asks me, "Jayde, do you want to help us out? We are going to separate the new clothes. We bought them at an estate sale."

"Yes, I would love to help. What should I do?" I ask.

For two hours, Marley, Sydney and I sort the clothes from the estate sale. We separate them by type, color and size. During that time, we talk about the store, vintage clothing and fashion.

My phone vibrates. I have a message from my sweet grandmother.

It's your sweet grandma. I'm home now. We're going to eat in fifteen (15) minutes.

"My grandmother is at home. We're going to eat in fifteen minutes," I say.

"Sounds good. Thanks, Jayde," says Marley.

Sydney takes the white jacket with the black buttons and hands it to me.

"This is for you, Jayde," Sydney says.

"I don't have the money to buy this," I say.

"It's a gift," Sydney says.

"I can't accept it," I tell her.

"It's for the work you did today," Sydney says.

"I just can't accept it," I say.

Sydney looks at me. She gives me the jacket and says:

"Jayde, it's obvious that this jacket makes you feel happy. You seem less unhappy. Take the jacket. You can work in the store for a few hours on Saturdays and you can take the jacket for your work today. Okay?"

"Oh! Alright. Thanks, Sydney. You're the best!"

Sydney and Marley are happy. I'm happy too.

I think about the jacket. And I think about the clothes I'm going to wear on Monday...

Chapter 3
The Comments

It's another week at my new school. I'm not very happy to go to school, but at least I have my new jacket.

"Jayde, are you going to eat breakfast?"

"Yes, sweet grandma. Thank you."

"The usual?"

"Yes, thanks."

Today, I'm going to wear my new white jacket with black buttons, black jeans and my black boots. Also, I'm going to wear a black cap. I really like this outfit.

I walk into the kitchen, and my grandmother is at the table with breakfast.

"Wow! Jayde, I like your outfit today. And the jacket?"

"It's new."

"Is it from Sydney's store? Folk Vintage?" asks my grandmother.

"It's a gift from Sydney. I'm going to work with her at the store on Saturdays. Is that okay?"

"Of course. At what time?" my grandmother asks.

"I don't know. In the morning maybe?"

"Ah. During the time I'm at the community center."

My grandmother volunteers at the Newport Community Center. She loves working with people.

"Grandma, one day I want to volunteer at the community center."

"I know, Jayde. You can when you're sixteen (16) years old…"

Hmmm. I have to wait… I'm only thirteen (13). I have to wait three (3) more years.

"Jayde, it's time to leave for school. I'm going to the community center. Do you want to walk with me?"

"No, thank you, grandma. I'll be there in a few minutes."

"Alright. See you after school."

"Bye, sweet grandma."

"Bye, Jayde."

I walk to school. Newport is small and my grandma's house is close to school.

*****

I arrive at school.

I'm in class, and I can hear the students talking about me.

"Look at that jacket. It's not a jacket from Under Armour."

"Look at those jeans. They're not from American Eagle."

"Look at those boots. They aren't boots from Aeropostale."

Later, I hear more students.

"That jacket is not from Under Armor, but it's an amazing jacket."

"Those jeans aren't from American Eagle, but they're fabulous."

"Those boots aren't from Aeropostale, but they're magnificent boots."

"So stylish!"

I say anything to the students, but I'm smiling.

Chapter 4
The Image in the Mirror

It's Saturday. I have to be at the Folk Vintage store at 10:00. I am going to walk. My grandma's house is on Bull Street, so the store is a little far away. The Google Maps app says I am going to have to walk for 20 minutes.

I don't want to arrive late, so I leave at 9:30.

It's May, but there isn't much traffic. Normally during the months May, June, July, August, and September, there is a lot of traffic in Newport. It is a destination for many tourists.

I enter the store. Today I'm wearing blue jeans and a yellow striped blouse. They are not fancy clothes. I'm here to work.

"Good morning, Sydney," I say.

"Hi, Jayde. Thanks for working today."

"I'm so happy. I really like the store. What are we going to do today?" I ask her.

"We are going to be doing a lot today. We have lots of new clothes from estate sales and used clothes from donations," Sydney tells me.

"Oooh! I want to look at everything!" I say to her.

Sydney and I go to the back room. There are a lot of clothes in big boxes. There are:

- shirts
- sweaters
- pants
- dresses
- skirts
- vests
- jackets
- shoes
- boots
- hats
- scarves
- hats
- T-shirts

And the clothes are all different colors and have a lot of designs. Wow!

"Look at the clothes!" I say.

"It's incredible, right?" says Sydney.

"What do we do first, Jayde?"

"Hm… maybe we should separate the clothes," I say.

"Yes! It is important to have a process. It is also important to speak with confidence," Sydney tells me. "Your opinion is important."

"OK. Thanks, Sydney. I'm going to separate the clothes in this box. Is that okay?"

"Sounds good."

For an hour, Sydney and I separate the clothes. We now have separate boxes for pants, shirts, jackets, sweaters, skirts, and dresses. In the skirts and dresses box, I see a long, dramatic dress. I take the dress and walk to the mirror.

I think, *What a wonderful dress! I want to wear it to school.*

"Do you like that dress, Jayde?" Sydney asks.

"Sydney, this is a dramatic dress. I love it," I tell her.

"Try it on. I'm going to open the store. I want to see you in the dress."

Sydney leaves the back room and goes to open the store.

I put on the dress and look in the mirror. I feel elegant.

Shortly after, Sydney comes to the back room where I am. She looks at me in the mirror.

"Oooh! Jayde! You are very elegant. You need to have that dress."

"Er, um... I don't know, Sydney. I love the dress, but..."

"Is it a question of money?" she asks me.

"Yeah. Yes…and no…," I tell her.

I think about the dress. It is long with a modern design and many colors. I feel free. Independent. And I feel more confident.

"If it's a question of money, I am paying you for your work here," Sydney says.

"It's not necessary, Sydney. I like to work with the clothes," I tell her.

"It is necessary, Jayde. You are helping me out a lot."

I look in the mirror again. I like the image.

"Can you pay me with clothes?" I ask. "Vintage clothes?"

"You like the clothes a lot, right?" Sydney asks me with a smile. "That's a good idea. I will pay you every two weeks. Is that okay?"

"Oh, yes! Thank you, Sydney."

A client enters the store. Sydney leaves the back room to go talk with the person. But first, I ask her a question.

"Sydney, can I take pictures of the clothes? I have an idea..."

"Of course! We'll talk about your idea later."

Chapter 5
A Video

"Bye, Jayde! I have to go to the community center early today. Your breakfast is on the table."

My grandmother is leaving early this morning. I will have a little time to be creative.

"It's okay, sweet grandma. Thank you."

"You don't want to be late for school."

"Okay, bye."

"Have a good day."

"Thanks, you, too."

I take out my phone and put all the photos of the clothes on TikTok. In a few minutes, I have an original and dramatic video of the clothes in the Folk Vintage store.

Wow, what a video! The clothes are magnificent, I think.

In the app, I add music and effects. At the end, I write:

- Do you want to be fashionable?
- Shop at Folk Vintage!

At the very end of the video, I add some hashtags and post it on social media in a new account. An anonymous account.

Ah! It's late. I have to go to school.

*****

It's time to go to school. I get a lot of likes on my post. Many people like vintage clothing. Or they like the video.

I enter school very happy. Today I'm wearing pink and yellow floral pants, along with a yellow sweatshirt. I also have a pink scarf and some big, gold earrings. The clothes are of all my favorite colors. They make me happy.

But there are comments:

"Look at those pants. Ugh! What awful colors!"

"Look at that sweatshirt. Ugh! It's the color of cotton candy."

"Look at the clothes. They're clothes you wear in the circus."

But there are other comments too:

"Oooh! Those pants are amazing."

"The sweatshirt is brilliant, and it looks comfortable."

"The clothes are original! I like them a lot!"

Before the first class of the day, there is a lot of excitement in the hallway. All the students are talking:

"Did you see the post on TikTok?"

"It's very original!"

"What a talent!"

"What is the name of the account?"

I look at the students' phones. Everyone is looking at MY post.

They think I'm talented. Ha, ha!

I walk to my first class, talented and happy.

Chapter 6
The Dress

It's Saturday, the day I work at Folk Vintage. I'm in the back room and Sydney is in the store when a person walks in.

"Hey, Syd."

It's Marley.

"Hey, Marley. How are you?"

"How are you, Sydney? I've seen a lot of the TikTok videos featuring the store. They're incredible!"

"Marley, you have no idea. Those videos are phenomenal! They are helping a lot. More people are visiting the store now," says Sydney.

"And you don't know who is creating the videos?" Marley asks.

"I have no idea. I want to know."

Sydney and Marley talk while I grab the fancy dress. I put it on. The dress is long and dramatic and has many colors. Once again, I feel free and independent. I have much more confidence.

Just then, Marley enters the back room.

"Oh!" I say, surprised. Marley sees me in the dress.

"Hello, Jayde," he says to me. "How are you?"

"Um…hi, Marley…"

"Jayde, you look very elegant in that dress," says Marley.

"Thank you," I respond.

Marley doesn't have any other comments.

But he has no negative comments either.

"Hey, come talk to us. We are talking about vintage clothing."

"Ok. In a minute. I need to change…" I tell him.

"Jayde, you look really good in that dress. Do you like it?" Marley asks.

"Yes, I love it."

"Do you want to wear the dress when you're not in the store?" Marley asks me.

"I would like to, but…"

"Jayde, you should wear the dress. It's very dramatic. I think it's an excellent dress for you."

"Yes, but…"

"What?" asks Marley.

"…I don't know," I say.

"Alright. If you want to walk around the store in the dress, great. If not, that's no problem."

Marley leaves the back room to talk to Sydney.

Can I wear this dress outside the store? I don't know… I think.

The dress IS elegant. It IS dramatic. And the colors are…

At that moment, I walk into the store with the dress on. Marley and Sydney's comments are positive:

"Jayde, you're beautiful."

"You look super elegant in the dress."

I have a big smile. I'm super happy.

"You have a pretty smile, Jayde," Sydney tells me.

"Thank you. I am very happy," I tell her.

"Jayde, why don't you wear the dress all day in the store?"

"Can I, Sydney? I'd love to. Thank you."

"You can also help with some photos of the clothes. I'm not very good at taking photos, but clearly, it's necessary..."

Marley asks, "Jayde, do you know about the TikTok videos? The videos of the store?"

I don't want to say anything. It's a secret.

"Videos?... No...," I tell him.

I think about some new ideas for videos. I want to be creative...

I read a poster in the store that has the reasons why buying vintage clothing is a good idea:

- to have different and unique clothes
- to buy good clothes at a lower price
- to buy more clothes for less money
- and... because it's fun 🙂

Aha! I have another idea for a new video.

Chapter 7
The Incident

"Oh, wow, Jayde," my grandmother says. "I like your outfit today. Those pants are phenomenal."

Today I am wearing a pair of bell-bottom pants with many different colors and designs, a black blouse and my black boots. I like my outfit.

"Thanks, sweet grandma. I like my clothes too."
"You have a good eye for fashion, do you know that?"

"I know! Ha, ha! But thank you. I like clothes and fashion a lot."

"I'm going to stop by Leo's Market after my work at the community center. Do you want to have something in particular for dinner?"

"No. Thanks, grandma. Bye. I'm going to walk to school."

I walk to school and think about the idea of a new video for the store. I'm going to need the help of my friend, Riley. We will make the video after lunch.

*****

Riley and I eat alone during lunch. She is a new friend.

"Riley, are you ready to make the video?"

"Yes, Jayde. You just want your clothes in the video, right?"

"Yeah. You can record the video in the app, okay?"

"Sure. What are you going to talk about in the video?" Riley asks.

"I'm going to explain why buying vintage clothing is a good idea."

"Ah. And what are the reasons?"

"The reasons are having different and unique clothes, buying well-made clothes at a lower price, buying more clothes for less money and…. because it's fun."

"Those are great reasons. I like them."

Riley uses my phone to record the video. She is recording the video when some students pass by us in the hallway.

- Oooh, Jayde. I like the look.
- Those pants are magnificent.
- Jayde, you're original.

I am super happy.

But soon after, other students pass by us in the hallway.

- Those clothes are awful.
- Those pants are ugly.
- Those clothes are not stylish.

One of the students grabs my shirt. The buttons come loose from the blouse and the blouse falls apart.

"Jayde! Are you okay?" Riley asks.

The students run down the hallway laughing.

Riley puts the phone in her pocket and helps me with my shirt.

I'm not happy anymore. I'm angry.

"Physically? Yes, I'm fine. Emotionally? No…" I tell my friend.

"Let's go talk to the counselor," Riley says.

"Good idea. Riley, do you have the video?"

Riley takes his phone out of her pocket.

"Oh no! The video posted."

"Ugh. It's not a good day."

Riley tells me, "Don't worry, Jayde. You can edit the video."

Riley and I walk to the advisor's office.

* * * * *

The advisor calls my grandmother. My grandmother arrives and talks to the advisor, Riley and me. My sweet grandma is not happy.

"Thank you for calling me."

"You're welcome, Ms. Salvador. Jayde can stop by my office whenever they want. Are you okay, Jayde?'

"Yes. Thank you."

"And Jayde…"

"Yes?"

"Those pants are spectacular. You have good taste," the counselor says to me with a smile.

"Thank you. I like them a lot, too."

My grandmother and I leave the school.

"Do you want to eat something, Jayde?" my grandmother asks me.

"Yes. Can we buy empanadas from Leo's Market?"

"Of course. Let's go."

Chapter 8
The Solution

It's another Saturday. I have to work at the store today. I'm happy about the job, but I'm not happy about the incident at school.

"Good morning, Sydney."

"Hey, Jayde. How are you today?"

"I'm not that good. I have problems at school."

"Ah. Yeah? Are they academic problems... or...?"

"Social problems; problems with other people."

Sydney doesn't say anything. She listens.

"There are some students who are mean to me. They don't like my clothes.'

Sydney doesn't respond. She listens.

"Yea, I'm different. I'm different from the other students..."

Now Sydney responds:

"Jayde, it's hard being a teenager. It's when people begin to learn who they are. And you are a strong person for having a different style."

"Thank you, Sydney. You're right, it IS hard being a teenager. And I am different. But I like to express myself through my clothes."

"Yes! And you have magnificent style!"

"I love clothes. And I love vintage clothes. I like to be original."

"It's obvious, Jayde. You are more confident when you wear clothes that you like."

"Am I confident? Really?"

"You are. It's your confidence that makes you original."

"Thank you, Sydney. You're a good person. What are we doing today?"

Just when Sydney is telling me what to do, Riley enters the store.

"Jayde!"

"Hey, Riley. Riley, this is Sydney."

"Hi, Riley. Jayde talks a lot about you."

"Nice to meet you, Sydney. Sorry for the interruption."

"No problem, Riley. It must be important…"

"Yes, it is important. Jayde, did you edit the video?"

"Ugh, no! Is there another problem?"

"No. There is a solution!"

Riley explains that many people saw the video and wrote comments.

"Ugh, no! Negative comments?"

"No, positive comments! The awful students are in the video and now they're the ones with problems at school. Ha, ha!"

Riley shows me her phone so I can see the positive comments.

Now Sydney speaks: "Wow, Jayde! Are you the one who is making those videos?"

"Yes, it's me. Sorry…"

"Sorry? It's NOT a problem. You have a good eye for videos. You are so talented."

Riley says, "Jayde is phenomenal with videos."

"Obviously," Sydney says. "I will pay you to make the videos."

"You don't have to pay me. It's fun for me."

Now Sydney is very happy. She says "I have an idea, Jayde. Can you help us, Riley?"

"Yes, I would love to," Riley says.

For a few hours Riley and I made a lot of videos of the clothes in the store. How fun!

Chapter 9
Confidence

For two weeks, Riley and I work on a lot of videos. I post every day on TikTok.

In the videos, I write messages like

- Do you want original clothes?
- Are you visiting Newport in July?
- Come visit us at the Newport Folk Festival!

Folk Vintage is going to be at the Newport Folk Festival. Sydney, Marley, Riley and I work hard. We prepare a lot for the event.

There's only one more week of school.

But today is an extra special day.

I enter the kitchen before leaving for school.

"Jayde, oh!'

I look at my grandmother, but I don't say anything.

"Jayde, oh!" my grandmother says again.

"Wow!"

I think about confidence. I have confidence. I will go to school with confidence.

"Jayde, you look beautiful. The dress is elegant, wonderful and spectacular. And you... you are magnificent."

"Thank you, my sweet grandma. I love it. The dress is fabulous. I feel so good. I love expressing myself through clothes."

"Now, eat something before school," my grandmother tells me.

I'm at the table eating my breakfast and looking at social media. I see a lot of great comments on my videos:

- These videos are fantastic!
- I love vintage clothing.
- Now I buy my clothes from vintage clothing stores.

And my favorite:

- The model in the videos is a natural and beautiful.

At that moment, I get a text message from Sydney:

> Jayde, can you stop by the store this afternoon? A man from Megapaca[1] wants to talk to you. He likes your videos. 😳

I answer:

> *What is Megapaca?*

Sydney writes:

> *Megapaca is an international company from Guatemala. It is a large used clothing company.*

I answer:

> 😳 *Wow. Why does he want to talk with me?*

---

[1] Megapaca: a second-hand clothing retailer founded in Guatemala.

Sydney writes to me again:

The man says he likes your videos.

I write:

Incredible!

With this information and new confidence, I walk to school in my wonderful dress.

Chapter 10
Fame?

It's the weekend of the Newport Folk Festival.

It's a three-day music festival at Fort Adams State Park.

"Jayde, can you put the shirts on the table?"

"Of course. Sydney, how many people are coming to the festival this weekend?" I ask her.

"Good question, Jayde. I don't know."

Marley says, "There are a maximum of 10,000 people each day."

"Excellent! "We're going to have a lot of work," I say.

"I hope so!" Sydney says.

"Jayde, which artist do you want to see this weekend?" Sydney asks.

"Oh, Jon Batiste! He plays tomorrow afternoon. I want to see him if it's possible."

"Do you like his music?" Marley asks.

"Yes, but I love his clothes. Ha, ha!"

"Have you heard his song, *Be Who You Are*?" Sydney asks.

I don't have time to respond. There is a group of teenagers running where I am. They have a lot of energy.

"It's them!"

"It's the famous Vintage Clothing model!"

"I want a selfie with them!"

I'm a little nervous. What should I do?

Sydney and Marley look at me with big smiles.

"Jayde, are you ready? You're famous. Your fans love you."

The teens are very happy. They think I'm famous.

I'm not famous.

I'm just me.

ABOUT THE AUTHOR

Jennifer Degenhardt taught high school Spanish for over 20 years and now teaches at the college level. At the time she realized her own high school students, many of whom had learning challenges, acquired language best through stories, so she began to write ones that she thought would appeal to them. She has been writing ever since.

Other titles by Jen Degenhardt:

Moviendo montañas | Déplacer les montagnes | <u>Moving Mountains</u> | *Spostando montagne*
La vida es complicada | La vie est compliquée | <u>Life is Complicated</u>
El verano de las oportunidades | <u>Summer of Opportunities</u>
Clic o no clic: la decisión final | Cliquer ou ne pas cliquer : la decision finale
El Mundial | La Coupe du Monde | <u>The World Cup</u> | *Die Weltmeisterschaft in Katar 2022 | La Coppa del Mondo*
Quince | <u>Fifteen</u> | *Douze ans*
El viaje difícil | Un voyage difficile | <u>A Difficult Journey</u>
La niñera | <u>The Nanny</u>
¡¿Fútbol...americano?! | Football...américain ?! | <u>Soccer->Football??!!</u>
Era una chica nueva
Levantando pesas: un cuento en el pasado
Se movieron las montañas
Fue un viaje difícil
¿Qué pasó con el jersey?
Cuando se perdió la mochila
Con (un poco de) ayuda de mis amigos | <u>With (a little) Help from My Friends</u> | *Un petit coup de main amical | Con (un po') d'aiuto dai miei amici*
La última prueba | <u>The Last Test</u>
Los tres amigos | <u>Three Friends</u> | *Drei Freunde | Les trois amis*
La evolución musical
María María: un cuento de un huracán | <u>María María: A Story of a Storm</u> | *Maria Maria: un histoire d'un orage*
Debido a la tormenta | <u>Because of the Storm</u>
La lucha de la vida | <u>The Fight of His Life</u>
Secretos | Secrets (French) | <u>Secrets Undisclosed</u> (English)
Como vuela la pelota

Cambios | Changements | Changes
De la oscuridad a la luz | From Darkness into Light |
Dal buio alla luce | De la obscurité à la lumière | Aus
der Dunkelheit ins Licht
El pueblo | The Town | Le village

@jendegenhardt9

@PuentesLanguage
World Language Teaching Stories (Facebook group)

Visit www.puenteslanguage.com to sign up to receive information on new releases and other events.

Check out all titles as ebooks with audio on www.digilangua.co.

59

ABOUT THE TRANSLATOR

My name is Matías Salazar. I am a 14-year-old boy who turns 14 in July. I am in 7th grade at Greenwich Country Day School. I am from Greenwich, CT and still live there. I like to play soccer and basketball with my friends. I want to grow up to be either A pro soccer player or play in the NBA.

Author's note: For those of you playing along at home...
Yes, this is THE Matías from the story, *El jersey*.

ABOUT THE STUDENT EDITOR

Lucas Gonzalez is an 11th-grade student from New York, West Nyack. He frequently writes short stories in his free time and loves Language Arts as a whole. Aside from his stories, Lucas enjoys watching various kinds of films to take notes and further improve the quality of his writing. Lucas has a wide array of skills when it comes to writing different kinds of stories and he loves to express them all in various forms of writing, be it poetry or short stories. He aspires to take his writing to the highest level it can possibly be in order to provide unique and touching stories for teenagers and adults alike to enjoy.